The Ultimate Fiction Thesaurus – Complete!

Sam Stone

Intro

There are a thousand ways to say something and at least a few hundred to express it well. This is not simply another thesaurus but a tool which aims to shave a year off of your creative development. This is a bold objective but as you go over these devices, in this brief but powerful tutorial, it will train your mind to think like a novelist. Let's see how this works:

First we start with a character description: Bill has grey hair.

This is a fine description, and certainly direct, but let's flex our creative muscle a little more:

Bill's hair is *salted* with grey.

Bill's hair is *frosted* with age.

Bill's hair is *threaded* with silver.

Now try these words on your own: *peppered, streaked, flecked, weeded*

You can immediately see the limitations of a traditional thesaurus; they are helpful at supplying a literal   equivalent, such as charcoal for grey, but frequently miss the finer nuances of language.

Beyond the inspirational support most books offer, I can assure you that two things, and only two, are guaranteed to improve your writing. These are reading and the act of writing itself. This is a unique literary thesaurus that bridges the gap of reading by taking common descriptive devices and words and places them into usable categories that will serve as a ready toolbox for your own writing.

Let's try another quick example and add a few more years to Bill's age:

Bill was old and wrinkled.

– This is somewhat vanilla, yes?

Deep furrows bracketed Bill's mouth.

– This works better because it's specific. And look at that really neat use of the word *furrow,* this is one of our concept words for aging.

This 'literary thesaurus' grew organically over years of focused reading and note taking. Sometimes I will provide concept lists and other times I'll provide examples of usage. So let's begin…

Character Study

The character will always dictate the descriptions that work or don't work, but it's important to remember that a character is more than a face and a body type. They have voices, expressions, and body language. Clothing is also a telling sign of occupation and social status.

BODY TYPES - FIT: *buff, strong, lean, slender, firm, wispy lanky, slim, sleek, delicate, six pack, dainty, sculpted, zero body fat, hard, tone, solidly built, stringy.* **FAT:** *well padded, plump, fleshy, heavyset, round, pug, pudgy, husky, chunky, massive, stubby, meaty*

CLOTHING- GOOD: *fancy, clean, matching, pleated, creased, understated, well heeled, pressed, fashionable, meticulous, smart, crisp, tasteful, subtracts age, showcases the best features.* **BAD:** *vulgar, disheveled, faded, irregular, worn out, tattered, dated, scruffy, dingy, filthy, shabby, drab, ratty, frayed, baggy, wrinkled, loud, fake, cheap, frumpy, poor fitting, busy, imitation, looking slept in.* **NEUTRAL:** loose fitting, familiar, comfortable, snug, outfitted in, attired in

ELDERLY - *stooped, leathery, weathered, hunched, sagging, gnarled joints, knotted joints, sagging skin, shaky hands, withered, knobby*

EYES - *dazzling, sad, educated, intelligent, piercing, alert, calm, almond shaped, beady, hooded, luminous, sallow, appraising, intense, heavily lidded*

FEMININE - *oval face, boyish figure, shapely, voluptuous, well endowed, high cheeks, ripe lips, jutting breasts, tiny, hourglass, narrow waist, curvy, alluring, broad hips, tapered legs, graceful, dainty, delicate, painted lips or nails*

HAIR - *swept, oily, combed, tangled, soft, brushed, ponytail, a halo of, a mane of, chopped, receding, braided, thin, fluffed, flipped, fussed over, tousled, teased, spiky, a mop of, glossy, sparse, wavy, cottony, untamed, unkempt, ringlets, finger combed.* **BEARDS:** *trimmed, stubble, fuzzy, scruffy, ragged, shadowed* *

MASCULINE - *hulking, burly, cleft chin, rugged, boyish, runty, puny, hard, coarse, raw boned, strong chin, rough hands, broad chested, husky, massive, powerful, large Adam's apple, calloused hands*

NOSES - *distracting, narrow, sloping, sharp, Roman, pug, broad, flat, aristocratic*

PERSONALITY - *pack rat, bad apple, set in his ways, down on his luck, a nondrinker, earnest, promising, good listener, practical, passionate, unscrupulous, knowledgeable, an only child, plain speaking, lacking social skill, eccentric, snooty, aristocratic, disgraced, tireless, bookish, scholarly*

SKIN – GENERAL: *pasty, ruddy, tanned, freckled, mole, scarred, dimples, pink, sun tinged, clear, blotchy, wind burned.* **OLD:** *furrows, fissures, smile lines, bagging skin, crinkle, sunken cheeks, lined, age lines, engraved, laugh lines, parenthesis around the mouth.* **YOUNG:** *smooth, unlined, lineless*

TEETH - *even, straight, pearly, crooked, chipped, unnatural, dentures, stained, perfect*

*You'll find that many descriptions of water will also lend itself to describing hair. For example, hair can be *wavy* or *flowing*; also, curls can *cascade* or *spill* down a woman's shoulders. So this is a very strong and effective connection in literature.

EXERCISE 1: No list is ever exhaustive. Add three new concept words for each existing category.

EXERCISE 2: Descriptive categories can lend themselves to other 'families' of nouns. Identifying this potential is important in your development. Reference your newly amended **CLOTHING** category and see how many of these adjectives would also serve as vivid descriptions for home furnishings, curtains, or other assorted linens.

EXERCISE 3: Create a new category titled **ODORS**, populating it with concept words like *perfumed and paralyzing.*

Voices

Yes, eventually your character will have something to say and his tone of voice will often transmit who he is or what state of mind he is in at a given moment, frequently the latter, and this is why I separated this group from our prior description keys...

soft spoken, whispered, grunted, muttered, murmured, grumbled, muffled, lowered voice, choked, half whisper, soaring, flat, chattered, croaked, even tone, stutter, hushed, bubbly, weak, rough, barely audible, snickered, hooted, clucked, curt, rumbled, urgent, howled, piercing, droned, hesitant, weary, out of patience, confidential, musical, monotone, rusty, oily, lisping, high, gravelly, soothing, brittle, strident, sharp, loud, raspy, nasal, groaning, husky, smoke cured, distorted, troubled, sputtering, braying, grating, stammering, strangled, toneless, an edge to his voice, wavy, urgent

That's a pretty deep list and it's good to remember that Bill can either *stutter* because he has a speech impediment or simply because his wife has caught him cheating with another woman. Most often the situation dictates the tone, which is a good introduction for our next stop...

Facial Expressions

ALERT - *intent, expectant, unblinking*

BORED *-glazed, tortured, listless, detached, dull eyes, flat eyes, remote*

COCKY - *contemptuous, arrogant, self-satisfied, pleased with himself, sure of himself, self-assured, aloof, confident, sly, an air of superiority, mocking, entitled, smirking, grinning*

DEFENSIVE - *stone faced, guarded, wary, defiant, mulish, cautious, reluctant, apprehensive, skeptical, cynical, distrustful*

DISPLEASED - *pinched, disgusted, horrified, annoyed, bristling, screwed up face, puckered face, withering gaze, a thin smile, pained, tortured, tolerant, dissatisfied, reproachful, sour, grim, disdainful, disappointed, put off, agitated, repulsed, stern, appalled, scowling, frowning, sore, detached*

HAPPY - *cheerful, satisfied, dopey, bubbly, giddy, glowing, energized, fresh faced, elated, merry, dreamily, amused, animated, soothing*

IMPATIENT - *listless, eager, keyed up, edgy, exasperated, distracted, annoyed*

MAD - *hard, stern, caustic, surly, ruffled, savage, hot, poisoning, menacing, stony gaze, moody, simmering, boiling, enraged, seething, sharp, defiant, glacial, icy, a black stare, scowling, glaring, glowering, stormy, berserk, sullen, fed up, harsh, venomous, cold, pinched, hostile, betrayed*

NERVOUS - *edgy, jittery, frazzled, grave, uneasy, wary, troubled, grim, frenzied, tense, worried, awkward, terrified, nauseated, keyed up, frowning*

NEUTRAL - *cloudy, non-committal, deadpan, unreadable, indifferent*

RELAXED - *calm, breezy, relieved, mellow, composed, subdued, pleased*

SAD - *bawling, long face, deflated, wistful, disconsolate, defeated, lifeless, remote, glum, forlorn, solemn, disheartened, regretful, morose, hysterical, hangdog, tearful, weary, blank face, sorrowful, grim, disappointed, grave, numb, anguished, wounded, despairing*

SHY - *plaintive, timid, downward gazing, disappearing*

SURPRISED - *cock eyed, stung, bewildered, gaping stare, sobered, stunned, numb, astonished, unnerved, overwhelmed, startled, unhinged, speechless*

THOUGHTFUL - *comprehending, shrewd, awareness, quizzical, curious, calculated, inquiring, puzzled, perplexed, confused, brooding, determined, haunted, stewing*

TIRED – *strained, wrung out, spent, fighting exhaustion, drained, fatigued*

CONDUITS OF EXPRESSION

There are nearly as many ways to conjure an expression as there are expressions themselves so don't limit your imagination to 'Bill looked tired'. Let's consider some other possible constructions of these expressions starting with our **TIRED** category:

a trace of weariness

a hint of fatigue

registered exhaustion

strain colored his features

And now try a few more words from our **NERVOUS** category:

a worried glance

an expression of concern

tension broke the surface

unease lined his features

EXERCISE 4: Construct three new conduits of expressions using these concept keys:

revealed, manner, evident, charged with, seemed, exhibited, was transparent, laced with, conveyed, betrayed, written, etched itself, displaying, adopted, a flicker of, brimming with, bore, flashed, an attitude of , wore

EXERCISE 5: Adoption is a necessary element of creative writing. Construct three new conduits of expression using vocal elements rather than facial expressions. Examples would be, *Bill's voice climbed with panic* or *Bill's voice carried a note of despair.*

EXERCISE 6: Smiles themselves are a deep well of expression, and not simply for happiness. Consider *a forced smile*, *a satisfied smile* or *a sly smile*. Plunder your brain for three additional possibilities.

Body Language

ANGER – *punching palm with fist, face burning, knotting hands, glaring, sweating, trembling, pursed lips*

EXERTION – *skin glistening, mopping a brow, complexion changing colors, labored breathing*

FEAR – *rigidness, dry mouth, closed throat, shaking, nail biting, heart thudding, shuddering, stiffening, fidgeting, cowering, holding one's breath, trembling, hugging one's self, retreating*

FLIRTING – *fluttering eyes, puckered lips, moistening lips, lips parting, making eyes at, climbing on toes for a kiss, crossing legs slowly, winking*

IMPATIENCE – *checking time, tapping foot, taking a deep breath, groaning, pacing, squirming, shifting in a seat*

INDICATING – *gesture toward, a sweeping gesture, point at, point with chin, angles eyes toward, signal, wave, motion to, nod at, draw attention to, draw a finger, hook a thumb toward*

RELAXATION – *laughing, stretching out, lacing fingers behind head, eyes softening, composing one's self, loosening neck, tucking legs beneath her, yawning, reclining, lounging*

SHYNESS – *averted eyes, scuffing shoe on floor, lowered head, flushed complexion, diminished voice, shrinking in one's chair*

THINKING – *chewing lower lip, hooding eyes, furrowing brow, temple one's fingers, drumming fingers, scratching temple, tapping a pencil*

WARINESS – *eyes returning to the same person or object (such as a door), looking side to side, glancing over one's shoulder, voice becoming hesitant, eyeing suspiciously, retreating a step*

EXERCISE 7: Review these list and identify body language that can serve multiple states of mind (listed or unlisted), then create a new category yourself titled **SLEEPY** and populate it with words like *nodding* and *blinking*.

This concludes our section on character study. If you feel as if you've been taking an acting course instead of a writing course, don't worry, it simply means you're embracing the concept that a fully realized character is not only well described but will successfully convey how he's processing the world.

VERBS FOR COMMON EVENTS

Let's talk briefly about descriptions. I hold a strong opinion that female authors tend to describe things in greater detail than their male counterparts. I suspect this split is rooted in the hard-wiring of the two sexes and women are more communicative by nature. Now this is a personal observation and it is less important that you agree or disagree with this thought than it is to approach your own reading with a focused eye that helps you define your own opinions about what makes a specific author, book, or even a paragraph, an engaging read.

This is an important concept because good writing is linked to studied observation and as you move further down the road of your literary journey, growing as a writer, you will begin to notice recurring patterns in the way authors construct ideas.

But descriptions are not limited to dressing up a noun. Great writing is most frequently linked to smart verb choices and just as we see patterns of familiarity in 'families' of nouns, reading also reveals literary patterns within verb selection. As you go over these concept keys, note the shades of color that differentiate the potential value of each word.

Dressing can be fairly specific to the type of clothing but a peek at these verbs reveal the wide range of creative possibilities available to you:

DRESSING: *Swaddled in a coat, stomp on boots, lace on shoes, shrug into a jacket, squeeze into a dress, tug on a shirt, slip into a coat, sling a purse over your shoulder, stuff into a coat, pull on trousers, step into pants, shoulder a bag, zipper into, wriggle into a dress, shove feat into shoes, wrap into a robe, cinch into a robe, gather into a robe, button into, pull on a sweater*

UNDRESSING: *peel off, strip, slip off, kick off, shuck, shed, wriggle from, work off, unbutton, unhook, unzip, unclip, shrug off, fight your way out* of, unshoulder

READING: *page over, peruse, skim, leaf through, scroll over, comb over, shuffle through, riffle the pages, consult, study, scour, scan, bury nose in, waded through*

WATCHING: focus on, fasten on, lock on, settle on, latch on, keep one eye on, train on, fix on, lit on, cling to, glue to, flit over, scrutinize, survey, examine, scout, gape at, ogle, gawk, leer

WRITING: *scrawled, doodled, jotted down, penned, penciled, labeled, inscribed, signed, notated*

SEARCHING FOR OBJECTS: *fumble for, loot, beat pockets, pat pockets, shuffle through, sift through, grope for, ransack, hunt, root through, feel around, prowl, scavenge, forage, poke through, trawling, plunder, rummage, prowl, pan the room for*

RETRIEVING OBJECTS: *fetch, fish out, swipe, extract, dig out, remove, dislodge, palm, scrounge, gather, snatch up, ransack, steal, collect, collar, ease it from, heft, score, catch, pinch, wrangle, appropriate, liberate, pry, draw, rake together, tug from pocket, scoop up, clutch, loot, scavenge, coax, accept, obtain, sweep up, haul out, paw at*

PUTTING OBJECTS AWAY: *pack away, stow, store, file away, plant, bury, shelve, zipper into a bag, secure, deposit, transfer, tuck away, discard, pocket, positioned, pile, park it, hang, squirrel away, cram into a closet, replace, hoist, shove, cart*

PROPELLING OBJECTS: *fling, sling, lob, wing, flick, heave, chuck, hurl, toss, sail it, rifle it, arc it, pitch, thrust, throw*

EXERCISE 8: Words have varying textures and tones. Women often *root* through a purse to find a lipstick. Consider the power of the word *forage* when searching for something to eat in a kitchen versus the word *trawling* when searching for a face in a crowd. Review the **RETRIEVING OBJECTS** category and identify those verbs which lend themselves to the retrieval of coins.

MOVEMENT

Movement is part of life and your characters will be doing plenty of it in any story you write. Bill can wheel his swivel chair from his desk to his file cabinet or race across town in a high speed chase. But again, having a number of choices is not only helpful but it can also serve to accentuate the mood of your character or the environment he's situated in. For example, when Bill's new secretary *bustles* into the office, it says less about her actual speed than the level of energy and excitement she is bringing to her new job.

FAST: *trotted, clamored, lunged, plunged, bolted, bowling, tore, jetted, hurried, sprinted, fled, squirted, hustled, flashed, darted, hurdled, flew, catapulted, sprang, blurred, thundered, bounded, scampered, dove, swooped, streaked, shot forward, scrambled, zoomed, scurried, chugged, overtook, sped, barreled, charged, rumbled, soared, hurled, burst through, rocketed, jogged, leapt, raced, bustled, skated, meteored, stormed out, surged*

SLOW: *plodded, trudged, dragged, poked along, crawled, slumped, crept, dropped back, lurched, lumbered, sluggish, edged toward, oozed, limped, gimped, hobbled, straggled, inched, trickled, moseyed, sloshed, waddled, waded, slouched, stiff*

NEUTRAL: *cruised, scooted, drifted, wandered, marched, bopped by, strode, flip flopped, peeled away, shuffled, glided, retired from, roved, bounced, scaled, negotiated, crisscrossed, floated, veered, hoofed, narrowed the distance, disappear into, clear out, stroll, hike, swagger, sachet, duck into, shamble out, set off, wafted, worked his way, breezed in, blew in, crested a hill, slipped past, boarded, sidle up to, prance, flutter, sail, skip, padded*

TURNING: *swing around, wheel around, spun, faced, whirled, swiveled, snapped around, angled toward, veered toward, rotated, circled, shifted, did a 180, wound, pivoted, screwed himself around, turned on his heel*

REST: *paused, halted, suspended, lingered, stopped dead, stand rooted, come to rest, freeze, hover, occupy, loiter*

Groups of people have their own distinct ways of moving and these examples will help solidify this concept...

GROUPS: *crowd a booth, pack an elevator, fill a bus, clear out, pile into, pile out of, troop toward, fan out, spill out, stream into, squeeze into, trickle from, form a procession, trail, gather, adjourn, assemble, migrate, leading, ushering, flock, jostle, circulate, congregate, team, herd, gather, mob, converge, flood*

Try these **AUTO** specific movements for fun:

peel off, roll to a stop, reach cruising speed, ease into traffic, nose into a parking place

The following two categories come in handy during the occasional moments of adventure. Physical conflicts are rarely graceful and it's helpful to remember **CLUMSINESS** works well in these situations.

CLUMSINESS: *topple, spill, stumble, slide, unsteady, wobble, careen, graceless, head over hills, flopped, steadying, sprawling, somersaulting, end over end, crashing, upended, recovered, weaving, canting, leaning on, staggering, sagging, spilling, swaying*

STEALTH: *moving in a crouch, sneaking past, crawling, moving along a wall, creeping, slipping past, tailing, a low dash, melt into a crowd, lurk, slink, get away clean, hunker, press himself against a wall, back track, prowl, slither, tip toe, corner, follow from a safe distance, stalk, retrace, dodge, sidestep, duck*

EXERCISE 9: *Mounted, scaled*, and *vaulted* are great variations for climbing stairs but only *vaulted* conveys a sense of urgency. Explore our **SLOW** category and identify words that would vividly illustrate movement through rain or snow.

EXERCISE 10: No category of description is ever limited to a single use. It is only limited by your imagination. Consider our concept keys for **CLUMSINESS** and list the words that could successfully describe varying states of illness, medication, or intoxication.

We are nearly at the end of the first study now but let's squeeze in two last stops before we go...

VIOLENCE

Try some of these verbs at your next barroom brawl:

FIGHTING – *claw, gouge, slash, damage, batter, smack, punish, lash, hammer, club, collide, collar, connect, pound, bean, tackle, slug, spear, knock senseless, swing, flail, punch, wrestle, bash, smash, pin, flail, throw a haymaker, slice, wrangle, ram, sting, stab, upend, kick, stomp, plow into, break, shake**

And sprinkle a little joy over the post-fight festivities:

BLOOD – *cakes, seeps, tastes, spurts, leaks, spatters, gushes through fingers, flecks, puddles, smears, soaks*

INJURIES - *lumps, limps, cuts, goose eggs, scars, splintered bones, spitting teeth, black eyes, limbs bending in impossible directions, opens gashes*

PAIN – *lasers, seers, spasms, racks, forces a scream, erupts, nauseates, unbearable, explodes, flairs, throbs, stirs, roars, radiates, sharp, stabbing, grips, jolt of, sting, dazes, hobbles, crumples, staggers, swells, blinds*

EXERCISE 11: No category of description is ever limited to a single use and damage can take many forms. Consider our concept keys for **FIGHTING** and list those words that could easily describe an auto collision.

EXERCISE 12: Speaking of damage… You'll find that many nouns are actually described in terms of ware or damage. Old things are best described this way. Consider: *battered, pocked, marred, faded, mangled, rusted, falling down, worn out, weak, tattered, cracked, neglected, distressed, dented, rickety, run down, wobbly, blistering paint.* Create two categories, **NEW** and **OLD,** and populate them with terms like *state of the art* and *vintage.*

And finally, a little noise…

SOUNDS

glasses clink, stools scrape, ice tinkles, pool balls click, silences stretch, stairs creak, planes and traffic drone, doors squeak, radios crackle, coughs rattle, keys jingle, bells chime, snow and gravel crunches, elevators ping, feet whisper over a floor, showers hiss, briefcases snap, neon buzzes, keyboards tap, rain pecks, tools clatter, intercoms squawk, metal clangs, newspapers rustle, guns stutter, halls echo, engines purr, jets scream

LOUD – *blares, sharp, shrieking, piercing, blasting, squalls, harsh, noisy, screaming, roar, clap, rumble, distracting, reverberating, resounding, hangs in the air, crashes, screeches*

QUIET - *barely audible, noiseless, out of earshot, diminished, muffled, hollow*

To this point we have really built our lesson around my own notes and observations but no decent tutorial would leave you without touching a few cornerstones of good writing...

UNIVERSAL TRUTHS

READ STRUNK AND WHITE: Besides being mercifully quick, The Elements of Style will refresh your grammar and help you write with more confidence.

SIMPLIFY: One of the most effective ways to improve a sentence is to condense your idea into fewer words. When a sentence isn't going well, I would encourage you to always return to NOUN + VERB, as in 'Bill ran', and then reconsider what constitutes an essential addition to this statement.

AVOID ADVERBS: If you slap a person, chances are you did it with a high degree of anger. So it is redundant to ever slap someone angrily or scream loudly. Adverbs rarely add anything of value and in their worst abuses can be distracting or even unintentionally comical. Improved verb selection will suppress the desire to modify verbs, so always think in terms of verbs and not adverbs.

SHOW, DON'T TELL: We have spent a great deal of time discussing the various ingredients of a character as well as the various manifestations of his mood. You will never have to say 'Bill was scared as he entered the cellar' if his heart is pounding as he descends the steps. Good descriptions always trump basic statements of fact.

ENGAGE THE FIVE SENSES: Nothing creates a stronger sense of setting than playing up those so small details that bring a place to life. If you're describing a salty margarita at a seaside resort or the stench of exhaust in a midtown traffic jam, you can be sure you have the scene clearly placed in the reader's mind.

WRITE DAILY: This is easier said than done and personally I think it should be amended to 'when possible'. Lives frequently include demands of career and family and your free time is not always best spent writing, particularly at the cost of fitness and good rest. That said, the more you write, the easier it is to prime the creative pump. Another consideration in this equation is the fact that some writing sessions are simply more productive than others and if you are tackling a long story, your best shot of pushing it to completion is to show up with a frequency that borders on obsession.

A Final Thought for Lesson 1

The best seller racks are populated with great authors. Many have backgrounds rooted in journalism, law, and advertising, so before they 'made it', they had already spent a great deal of time searching for better ways to express themselves. Their livelihoods depended on it.

Fortunately these careers are not a prerequisite to competent writing but there is a price to pay; thousands of hours of reading, writing, and self-editing are still ahead of you, but the pleasure you'll receive from this growth is well worth the investment.

When you read, read with pen and paper at your side and scratch down the words and sentences that leap from the page. As time passes, patterns will emerge and you will develop a heightened sense of all the tools and possibilities language has to offer.

It's been my pleasure to spend this time with you and best of luck with your writing.

*

Lesson II

Intro

Beyond the inspirational support most books offer, I can assure you that two things, and only two, are guaranteed to improve your writing. These are reading and the act of writing itself. **The Ultimate Fiction Thesaurus II** is a unique literary thesaurus that bridges the gap of reading by taking common descriptive devices and words and places them into usable categories s that will serve as a ready toolbox for your own writing.

Let's see how this works...

First we start with a description:

The morning was sunny.

This is okay, in fact sometimes simple is best, but let's give it another swing:

A *shaft* of light pierced the window.

Sunlight *flooded* the bedroom.

An easterly sun *streamed* into the kitchen.

Now try a few of these other lighting concepts on your own: **dappled, beat down, glinted off, streaked, filtered, drenched**

You can immediately see the limitations of a traditional thesaurus; they are helpful at supplying a literal equivalent, such as sunlit for sunny, but frequently miss the finer nuances of language.

Let's try another quick example and this time we'll ruin our perfect day:

The morning was thick with fog.

This clearly conveys an idea but with a little effort we can improve this description also.

The morning was ***shrouded*** in fog.

Fog ***settled*** like a blanket over the city.

I cheated on this last example, using not one but two words frequently associated with fog, the second being ***blanket***.

The **Ultimate Fiction Thesaurus II** is a continuing study of common literary ideas that underpin modern fiction. Sometimes I will provide concept lists and other times I'll provide examples of usage.

So let's begin…

Settings

Settings are an essential part of any story. In fact some settings are so important they can be mistaken for a secondary character. Think about Anne Rice's vivid depictions of New Orleans in The Vampire Chronicles or Charles Frazier's Appalachian Trail in Cold Mountain. Your own setting may not carry this weight of importance but your reader will still expect a world they can see, navigate, and recognize.

WEATHER CONDITIONS:

RAIN - swelling drainage ditches, rain streaked windows, smell of rain in the air, blurred glass, lashes, pecks, dwindles, breaks, thunder rolls, lightning crackles, rain coming at you sideways, empty sidewalks, lapped, churning clouds, streams in the road, gloomy, trickles, hampered by rain, muggy, shrouded by rain, spray of water, sky turns dark, clouds threaten, objects gleam, glisten, huddle under an umbrella, shake off the rain, overflow, shower, dribble, rain slanted, steam rose, splash

WIND - flapped, squalled, drifted, stirred, stinging, blowing debris, violent, trickles as a breeze, whispers, moans

SNOW - blankets, covers, can't get warm, clings to clothes, slows driving, enchants, children at play, shoveling driveways, dressing in layers, crystalizing breath, chimneys smoking, snow crunching underfoot, icicles dripping

HOME INTERIORS:

GOOD – modern, charming, spacious, inviting, tidy, warm, meticulous, a sanctuary, upscale, homey, bright, refurbished, lush carpet, handsome, ornate, solidly built, polished wood, intricate detailing, graced by, generous ceiling, handcrafted, gilded, clean, upscale, renovated, awash in light, brushed nickel, neatly arranged, artful, high end

BAD – dank, dark, lifeless, aging, cramped, musty, dilapidated, rundown, dripping faucets, peeling wallpaper, loose boards, shoddy craftsmanship, mismatched furnishings, carpet stains, drafty, gloomy, naked bulbs, flickering lights, low rent, stark walls, musty, sagging roof, plain, squalid, crudely crafted, no frills, cheerless, water rings on furniture, cold, deserted, unadorned, bowed shelves, cigarette burns

YARDS & EXTERIORS – shaded by oaks, shielded by shrubs, hemmed by a fence, undergrowth, graced by a willow tree, a stand of trees, grass sprouting, a footpath, a slate path, flood lights, terraced, dotted with boulders, dirt encrusted, ivy trellis, landscape stretched, a screen of oaks, weedy, swimming pool, patio, wood deck, hilly, sloping, in need of water, basketball goal in the driveway

LOCATION IN REALTION TO OTHER LANDMARKS – hugged the river, squeezed between, sandwiched between, situated on, hemmed by, bracketed by, bordered by, flanked by, clinging to, dotting the hills, ocean side, extending the length of, by the airport

EXERCISE 1: No list is ever exhaustive. Add three new concept words for each existing category.

EXERCISE 2: Create a home, specify its location, and describe its physical responses to outside weather conditions.

EXERCISE 3: Create a new category titled **ARCHITECTURAL FEATURES** and populate it with concept words like *crown molding* and *bay windows.*

We've reviewed a number of physical attributes to setting and placement, but let's not forget another very important aspect of all events...

TIME

Stories work best when events are presented in chronological order. You shop, you cook, and then you eat. This flow is organic to life and thus each scene props up the trailing situation.

Perhaps your story is experimental or you welcome the challenge of a non-linear narrative ... I say, go for it. Great writers routinely bend ideas to their vision and you will grow for the effort.

That said, if you choose simplicity over challenge, you will still have memories and backstories to contend with. One of the easiest ways to portray a past event is to have your characters express it themselves in conversation.

My personal taste is such that I prefer dialogue over narrative but a more objective analysis of this choice promotes two strengths: 1) Dialogue will prevent you from carrying on too long and losing the more immediate relevance of NOW, and 2) Dialogue is the way we generally experience the lives of others. You know your son had a bad day at school because he told you his teacher caught him cheating on a math exam and not because you had the luxury of climbing into his head and seeing each detail as it unfolded.

Another method to recall the past is to introduce a memory trigger such as an old song that reminds our hero of the summer he met his spouse.

So the bottom line? Any chronological method you choose is valid so long as it achieves clarity for the reader.

Before we move on...

Give Your Wristwatch a Rest:

With a little creativity an hour can become *a miserable hour later* or five minutes can happen *in five minutes flat,* but let's try a few alternative concepts for passing time:

never-ending, when the tea was gone, on the fly, the food went cold, split second timing, up with the sun, there in two strides, buying time, smoking his third cigarette, shortly, the days piled up, a beat passed, seldom, rare, later than usual, just as, just after, wasting no time

Hopefully you are seeing this fictional world more clearly now... But what about your character?

Perception

Every art form has a guiding set of principles and there is no greater principle for fiction than 'Show, Don't Tell'. The best way to 'Show' is to keep the five senses active and engaged.

SOUND - reverberates, echoes, whispers, creaks, distracts , spills from the kitchen, whirs, footsteps fade down the hall, garble, rattle, jangle, chatter, rustle, click, grumble, grunt, diminish, brittle, flat, mingles with, buzzes, groans, squeaks, clip clops, screams, blares, shrieks, chimes, tinkles, hisses, pings, hums, thunks, whistles

SMELLS – wafted in the air, tinged the air, scented the room, hung in the air, drifted, aromatic, reeked, rank, musty, floral, perfumed, paralyzing

TASTE – FOOD: stale, scarfing, bland, bad aftertaste, savor, flavorless, attacked his lunch, nibbled, consumed, spear it on a fork, cold, bitter, sweet, spooned, smothered in ketchup, appetizing, cheating on a diet, charred, munched, salted, crammed, plunge a spoon in, rich, melt in your mouth, crunchy.

TASTE - DRINK: tasted, sipped, swigged, slugged, nursed, pulled on the bottle, threw back, took a draw, drained his glass, glugging, toss back, chugged, dipped into, washed it back with, polished off, gulped, downed another, turned the bottle up, emptied the glass, sucked

TOUCH – finger, fingers skate over, fingers outline, fingers trace, fingers close around, fingers linger over, fingers graze, fingers crawl over, hooked fingers around, dig into, pinch, chaff, soothe, knead, massage, probe, paw, scratch, burn, cut, sting, warm, tingle, rough, smooth, silky, coarse, gritty, slimy, damp, lumpy, stroke, rake

VISION – peer at, scrutinize, survey, scan, spot, examine, scout, gaze, study, focused on, fasten on, lock on, settle on, rest on, latch on, eyed, trained on, fix on, lit on, eyes clung to, glued to, flitted over, took a long look at, eyes bore into, gape at, gawk at, strain to see, ogle, leer, penetrating stare, consulted, targeted, glance over, observed , regard

And since we are on the subject of his visual perception, let's give the color wheel a spin...

COLORS

There are a number of self-help books dedicated entirely to the study of hair and eyes and I imagine these books spend a fair amount of time speaking about color. But color is everywhere and it's almost always helpful to add a poetic flare to these adjectives. I suggest looking to nature first, particularly its gemstones. That said, I suggest caution when considering these devices for eyes. A fabulous shade of wallpaper or fabric is one thing but this form of character attribution may strike your reader as false, overly romantic, or just plain smarmy. So be sure your 'improvements' are not distracting.

Black – inky, raven, ebony

Blue – flinty, deep sea, topaz

Brown - chestnut, smoky brown, terracotta, sandy

Gray – slate, charcoal, marble

Green – emerald, jade, summery green, leafy green

Orange – tangerine, amber

Pink – coral, cotton candy

Red – ginger, wine, ruby, strawberry, garnet

White – lily, ivory, wedding cake white

Yellow – blonde, golden, tawny, honey

Neutral Modifiers – tinged, vivid, metallic, Technicolor, muted, cheerful , neon

And Speaking of Color and Eyes…

Novelists adore violet eyes but this trait is extremely rare in people. If realism is your goal, I suggest staying around blue, brown, gray, green, or hazel and simply adjusting the tone. For example use light, medium, or dark brown eyes. You can also mix colors. For example: gray-green eyes.

Still searching for that little extra something? Try adding an adjective: *luminous* gray-green eyes. The Ultimate Fiction Thesaurus offers a number of additional suggestions for eye modification, including *expressive*, *intelligent*, and *piercing*.

EXERCISE 4 – Smart verb choices not only identify the action but they also convey the urgency or intensity of that action. List three **VISION** words that would be useful for locating a name in a phone book.

EXERCISE 5 - Taking this idea a step further, verbs can also relay significant information about the character's attitudes, intelligence, or intentions. List two **VISION** words for a lawyer reviewing a legal contract, and then list two more for a spoiled rock star reviewing the same contract.

EXERCISE 6 - Touch supplies texture but it also conveys human emotion. Create a subcategory for **TOUCH** titled **RELATIONSHIPS** and populate it with concepts like *caress*, *nuzzle*, and *cuddle*.

EXERCISE 7: Our five senses are a terrific place to shop for the memory triggers I mentioned in **TIME**. Review the perception concepts and create three memory triggers.

As your hero moves from location to location to experience this world, chances are good he'll do a fair amount of driving to get there. Let's take a minute to study the language devices surrounding this common activity.

DRIVING

ACCELERATION: press down the accelerator, engine whines, floored it, gunned the gas, flatten the gas pedal, darted, growled up the avenue, shot forward, engine strained, peeled off, roared, closed the distance, sped toward, bearing down on, squash the gas, speedometer needle nudged to seventy, surged ahead, squeal off, broke the speed limit, goosed the pedal, streaked by, tires smoked, tore around the corner, picking up speed, closed the gap, revved, leaned on the gas, fed gas to the engine, smoke pours off tires, tromped, jockeyed, spray of gravel, trail of dust

SLOWING: bark of tires, shriek of brakes, drew up, broke hard to a stop, crept past, gradually, poking along, abrupt stop, skidded to a stop, screeched to a stop, glided to a stop, pumped the brake, reduced speed, squeal of brakes, crawled, slid to a stop, yielded, pulled to a stop, stood on the brake, leaned on the brake, downshifted

CRUISING: roved, steered, on route to, driving west along, trailing, scooted, wheeled, glided, held it steady at 55, picked up the turnpike, cruised, convoyed, switched lanes, motor purred, prowling, piloted, caravan

TURNS: negotiated, maneuvered, a curving right, a sweeping left, veered, executed, steered, made a sharp right, an illegal U-turn, angled for, cut the wheel, banked toward, swerved, bore right, turned a corner, cornered, wheeled left, cranked the wheel, blinking signal

TRAFFIC: weaving in and out, wound through an opening, worked his way, nosed into, swung into, horns blare, evenly spaced, a cop directing, snarled, inched forward, rush hour, wait for a light, narrow streets, lean on the horn, speed bumps, cut in front of, zipped into, a knot of cars, strangle of traffic, clogged, drone of traffic

HAZZARDS: speed bumps, closed streets, one way streets, bouncing over potholes, rattle over train tracks, potted with holes, skid, careen, swerve, jounce, fishtail, spin out, leapt curve, went airborne, an abrupt bend, punctured tire, flipped end over end, found traction, slick tires, a light loomed ahead

STEALTH: tail, fall in behind, swung in behind, monitored traffic in his rearview, followed at a safe distance, circled the block

After all of that, your hero should be thankful to arrive in one piece...

PARKING: nose into a space, park at a hasty angle, crunch of gravel, aisle of cars, stopped curbside, parked in the shade, steered to the curb, moved onto the shoulder, cut the engine, killed the engine, pull into, pull up, park well away from, eased in between, left the motor running, zipped into, idled, fed a parking meter, put it in park, dropped him off

EXERCISE 8: Adoption is a key to successful writing. Review the **TIME** concepts in **Give Your Wristwatch a Rest** and create two new concepts for passing time during travel. For example: *a short distance later*. If you get stuck, look for inspiration around the needle of your fuel tank.

EXERCISE 9: Groups have their own distinct ways of moving. Review the **CRUISING** category and identify two examples of this concept.

Now speaking of worlds in motion, we spent a fair amount of time talking about **MOVEMENT** in **The Ultimate Fiction Thesaurus.** The flip side of all of this stirring about is to let your hero just kick back and rest.

SEATING

SITTING: sprawl out, recline, slouch into, squeeze next to, settle, slide onto a stool, drop into, a vacant chair, straddled, placed his rear in, raked a chair across the floor, scraped a chair under him, lowered himself, lounged, offered a chair, draped himself onto, curled up, hops up on, perched, stretched out on, eased into, tumbled into, collapsed into, sank back, parked in, hoisted himself onto a stool, slumped into, planted, flopped down, poured herself into, drew up a chair, motioned him to sit, ordered to sit, encouraged to sit, relax into, topple into, fell heavily into, sag into, spill into

RISING: slid off barstool, knocked back chair, exploded from, got to his feet, pulled himself out of, came up, dusted off the seat of his pants, pushed back, uncoiled from, left dent in cushion, reared up, struggled to his feet, hauled himself up, swung legs down, sprang up, slipped off, tipped his chair, shot up, heaved himself, was off his chair, pulled her to her feet, fought to get to his feet, started up, hoisted, shoved back

SHIFTING: wheeled, swiveled, rolled, stretched for, spun, scooted chair forward, crossed legs

It's those verbs again, isn't it? … You bet.

EXERCISE 10: Smart verbs relay information about your character. Provide three concepts word from **SITTING** to describe a depressed young widow.

EXERCISE 11: Frequently descriptions can lend themselves to related ideas. Identifying this potential is critical to your development. Example: **depression = (fatigue) = aging**. Now review your answers from EXERCISE 9 and see how many of the selected concepts would work equally well for the widow's elderly neighbor.

EXERCISE 12: Now engage the senses. Revisit **SOUNDS** and identify words that would support a description of our elderly neighbor rising from his chair.

We are nearly at the end of the study now but let's squeeze in a few last stops for fun...

SMOKING

Tear plastic from pack, tap out, flick the wheel of a lighter, scrape a match, cup the flame, wave out a match, smell of sulfur, drew on, pull on, puff, take a drag, flick ash, savor, cough, glowing tip, reek, stale, stub out, crush, erase, snuff, ground out, smothered

Clouds: a ring, halo, wafted, tendrils, ribbons, shrouded in, hangs in the air, billows, snakes from, smolders, pours, engulfs, coils

DRINKING

Since **TASTE** included some really nice verbs for drinking let's take a quick look at some other language sure to wet your whistle...

POURING AND SERVING: added a splash of, freshened, found himself a drink, uncorked, refilled, measured, brimming, plunked ice cubes in, speared an olive, armed himself with, doctored his coffee, warmed his coffee, broke the seal, stopped the bottle, untwisted the cap, tightened the cap, uncapped, added a slice of lemon

BAR RELATED NOISES: clink of glasses, scrape of stools, rattle of ice, pool balls clicking, jukebox playing in the corner, empty bottles crashing into a trash bin, the band warming up, patrons growing louder

And if you love a little adventure nothing goes better with drinking than the old bang-bang. So this will fit nicely with the **VIOLENCE** section we created in the Ultimate Fiction Thesaurus...

GUNS

touched the trigger, winged, stepped over the body, dug the gun in his back, moving in a crouch, sighted the gun, punctured, weapon of choice, carried the gun low, spent cartridges, tightened hand around grip, look for cover, bullet glanced off, peppered, a hail of fire, stitched holes, blew out windows, whiff of sulfur, bulged beneath his shirt, tore through, leveled the gun, caught one in the arm, directed her with a gun, backed him down with a gun, knuckle whitened around trigger, drew the pistol, cleared the pistol, used as a shield, finger tightened, spat fire, flash of gunfire, held with both hands, gun bucked, finished him

SOUNDS: shot reverberated, roared, erupted, rang, echoed away, exploded, bullets shrieked, stutter of gunfire

To this point we've built our lesson around notes and observations about specific language use. Now let's step back and look at some of the big picture challenges for fiction.

Inspiration – For me, the best ideas arrive away from the work and the best details arrive at the keyboard. Watch and read things that inspire you. Try a little 'method writing' too; it's sort of like method acting. For example, if your hero likes spending time in his garage, try changing the car oil yourself. These devices rarely supply great revelation but they do help center your mind.

Writers Block – There are two places this can happen, when choosing a project or writing in mid-work.

Choosing the wrong project can frequently mean sinking valuable time into a void of nothingness. Sounds pleasant, doesn't it? Don't panic. I find most projects with no real future establish this status early. Allow yourself the freedom to write multiple test chapters and search for the project that's right for you.

Stuck in mid-work? Inspiration will always download ideas at its own pace so don't wait. Spend this time editing prior chapters. Also, if you have a general idea of locations that you will need later, begin building these sets. They have the potential of sparking ideas and you will be grateful to have started them when you finally reach that section.

Time Management – Don't cram all of your free time into a single day or weekend. Try to write a little every day and plan your week around this goal. Other goals are good too, some people like word counts and others like deadlines. These devices can force you to march ahead but it's good to know your limits and needs. For example, I love writing but I also love football, so fall isn't particularly productive for me… And I'm okay with this. In short – Be a kind boss.

When to Stop Editing - There are actually two very good places for this:

On a current project - Stop editing when it accomplishes less than adding new material.

For a retired project – Stop revisiting old projects when you are distanced from that work by either time or inspiration. You may be a better writer at forty than you were at thirty but it's important to remember that you are not the SAME writer. Frequently it's the early works of artists that fans enjoy most, so my vote is firm on this - Leave the crude energy as it is.

A Final Thought

The premise behind writing these companion studies was to help bridge the gap of reading. There is no such bridge for writing. Writing is the long journey of one and it comes at a very high cost. You steal time away from every other aspect of your life to sit down a few hours each week and put ink to page. This devotion does not merit feelings of envy, frustration, self-loathing, or self-doubt. Nor does it ever require the endorsement or validation of others.

Respect the process. Respect your authorship. Write.

*

Made in the USA
Lexington, KY
15 September 2014